Betrayal, Sorrow and Tomorrow

Poems about the effects of divorce on you, your spouse and your children

CHRIS F. WOLLINKS

authorHOUSE®

AuthorHouse™
1663 Liberty Drive, Suite 200
Bloomington, IN 47403
www.authorhouse.com
Phone: 1-800-839-8640

First published by AuthorHouse   10/20/2008

ISBN: 978-1-4343-9027-1 (sc)
ISBN: 978-1-4343-9028-8 (hc)

Printed in the United States of America
Bloomington, Indiana

This book is printed on acid-free paper.

INTRODUCTION

Divorce, I have come to surmise, is never a pleasant experience, not for me, not for the spouse, and certainly not for the children. Avoiding divorce, the Big D word, should be encouraged at all cost. Divorce is devastating—emotionally, socially and financially. It is, to use the adjectives of the poem on Page 19, appalling, betrayal, disgraceful, humiliating, lonely, anguish, grief, remorseful, sorrow, and traumatizing.

The betrayal, whether you or your spouse caused it, is like a heart attack to the human body. The betrayal, whether caused by infidelity, neglect, abuse or any other reason why marriages fail, is there and you must deal with it. If you committed the infidelity, you feel sorry for what you have done. If you feel neglected or mentally abused, something happened along the way. What happened? How thoughtful were you, did you have anything to do with causing him to neglect you? Did you have anything to do for causing her to be mentally cruel to you? Incidentally, there is no excuse for physical abuse.

When your marriage breaks up, you feel like you want to die and give up. You ask yourself, "What did I do?" You start blaming and hating yourself for destroying a family, for hurting your spouse and hurting your innocent children. You tell yourself that the children do not deserve this—and they do not.

When you are betrayed, you question what you did to deserve this. You wonder what you could have done to prevent it. What were the signs that you overlooked? What did you do wrong? Why did she do it? You are resentful, hateful, vengeful and feel that the end of the world is at hand.

You start to question what drove you or your spouse away. Maybe it is just that you grew apart--not tending to each other's needs. You stopped talking to each other in a meaningful way. You stopped having intimate, romantic moments. You put on a few extra pounds. Something happened to set you apart.

The feelings for each other have faded or are fading. You try, or at least you think you have tried to work through your problems. You feel your partner is uncooperative in the reconciliation efforts. You feel choked.

I have lived through all these sentiments and I have put my feelings in poetry. I used it as therapy to get through the emotional tides that I felt and that you may be feeling now. I have written these poems to help myself cope. I am publishing them to help you cope.

I have also written poems to help the children cope. Children are the innocent victims in a divorce, caught in the middle. The father and mother are each trying to pull the children to sympathize with them exclusively. The children hear one thing by one parent and then innocently they repeat it to the other parent, only to bounce back and cause more agony for both parents and the children—making the children torn in half. Children are not a tennis ball to bounce back and forth between parents. They are sensitive and innocent little human creatures who had nothing to do with the break up of their parents. Yet, their emotions are battered like a baseball in extra innings.

The emotions come in stages. First, you feel betrayed, hurt, sorrowful, angry, and resentful. Then the feeling turns to apologetic, loneness, spirituality, forgiveness, remorseful and a desire to do anything to make things right. In my case, I tried very hard to keep the family together, to keep the nineteen-year-old marriage vibrant. I suggested a romantic vacation to Paris. No, was the answer—too busy. I suggested marriage counseling. "No!" was the answer. I asked my then spouse to see a doctor. Yes! Yes! but the appointment was never made. I sent our priest, our good friend and my most respected elder in my family. They were not accepted.

I then gave up. I did all I can. I started thinking about tomorrow.

My poems then turned to my future. At 44, I could not live the rest of my life alone without a soul mate. My poetry writing therapy then turned to analyzing the meaning of love. How would I know who my soul mate is? What do I desire? What would be compatible to me? What would I want from the potential mate?

I answer these questions in the last part of the book by expressing that the mutual feeling of heart and mind must come together and agree on the person. For if you have desires for a person and your mind knows that that person is not for you, then you only have infatuation. Love cannot live on infatuation alone. In addition, if you have mutual goals and concerns and can understand each other but the love is not there, then you only have a friendship.

Your heart and mind must come together and agree. There must be love and friendship.

I hope my poems inspire you to keep your marriage strong. I hope that if your thinking of being unfaithful before you read my poems, then I hope to inspire you not to do it. I hope that you do not get to the last part of my book, I hope that you rekindle the love with your spouse and you have no need for finding another romance. I hope I have helped you.

To protect my children and to avoid any problems with my ex-spouse, I have not used my real name in this book. I think you can understand. In fact, I have used a pen name which does not suggest whether I am the wife or husband in the failed marriage. I have done this because the message is to both the husband and wife. I did not want the reader to think either my ex-spouse or I was at fault—actually I believe that we were both equally at fault, although my ex-spouse may still feel otherwise.

The pictures of the people in the book are depictions of everyday ordinary people from all walks of life and were not drawn or sketched to reflect or resemble any person, living or dead. Any reflection or resemblance to any person, living or dead, is purely coincidental and accidental and not done in any intentional or non-intentional manner. While some pictures show a man corresponding to a particular poem or theme in a poem, the picture could have been sketched to reflect a woman rather then a man. Nothing in these poems or the pictures should give anyone the impression that any one gender is more to blame for the break-up of marriages.

The pronouns referring to the husband and the wife in any poem could be interchanged. Any poem referring to the husband as the "bad guy" can be easily converted with the change of a pronoun to make the wife the "bad gal."

Finally, I would like to acknowledge the help and assistance of Jana Pivkova, who drew the illustrations for the book. While I suggested the types of pictures, it was her artful hands that brought the poems to life. I am forever indebted to her for her talent.

I also want to thank Abeer, I can't give her last name because it's the same as my real name. Thus, many readers may then know me and my identity, as much as I have tried to hide it, will be revealed. Abeer graciously helped with the editing of the book. I needed her help from a fresh perspective and she certainly offered that. Thanks Abeer.

Maybe I should thank my ex-spouse. Had my ex-spouse not filed for divorce and not carried the divorce through judgment, then I would not have gone through the many years of hurtful emotions and I would not have written these poems. However, to tell you the truth, the satisfaction of having published this book can never erase the pain that my ex-spouse has caused and cannot make the suffering that I have endured in the past several years escape my mind, especially the pain that I saw in the eyes of my children. So thanking my ex-spouse is not such a good idea.

While I love where I am at right now, I wish I had not been given the opportunity to write this book.

Chris

Table of Contents

Part III   Tomorrow

Safa   She Is the One

Part I

Betrayal

The Senses Tell It All

What are you doing woman?
Sure, you can feel the love gone
Sure, you can smell that unknown perfume
Sure, you can tell the touch is gone
Sure, you know he does not listen anymore
Sure, you can see he does not care
But what does your mind conclude?
There must be something wrong!
What are you doing to drive him away?
Have you forgotten how to feel?
Do you go to bed without that scent?
Have you lost that loving touch?
Are you nagging him to ignore you?
Do you not see your driving him away?
What are you going to do to keep him home?
Sense the atmosphere around you
Know what you can do to keep him around
Give that hugging feeling
Smell pretty for him
Touch him with affection
Listen and he will listen too
See him for what he can be

What are you doing man?
You feel something new
You smell something different
You touch something soft
You listen to someone warm
You see someone pleasing
But what does your mind conclude?
There must be something wrong
What have you done to drive her away?
What happened to that honeymoon feeling?
Have you bought her her favorite perfume?
Do you touch her with love?

Are you listening to her needs?
Don't you see that you are running away?
What are you doing to stay home?
Arouse her senses around her
Know how to keep her around
Feel what she is feeling
Buy her that perfume that arouses you
Touch her with love
Listen to her needs
See her the way you used to see her

Count Your Blessings

Wow! Your eyes perk
Over there you sneak a look
You have not felt that way
Since way before today

Before the day you said I do
I do to the one that made two
Into one being, one body
Now you are looking at somebody

Somebody other then your wife
To your wife you promised your life
But that somebody will destroy everything
Everything that means anything

Do you go over to her and flirt
Flirt with her in that mini-skirt
Skirting your life away
As your thoughts go astray

Stop and think
Have another drink
Relax and give thought
A lesson taught

Your blessings you should count
And do not have any doubt
A moment of pleasure
Is not worth the measure

Measure all you have built thus far
And get out of that bar
Go back home and make amends
And do not be that arrow that bends

So Foolish

How could I be so foolish?
Having the greatest mate
I made a most horrendous sin
I destroyed a family

How could I be so foolish?
Whatever the reason for my sin
The guilt eclipses the pleasure
I destroyed myself

How could I be so foolish?
I cry myself to sleep
I wake up alone
I destroyed my life

How could I be so foolish?
I tell you do not do it
Do not commit the ultimate sin
Do not destroy your life

THE HAND THAT NEEDS COUNSELING

So you raised your hand
And whipped it across like a band
Big man that you are
Are you feeling like a star?

Look at you now all alone
Lying in bed with a cold stone
That look you have upon your face
Shows a destroyed family without their ace

You blew off steam
Now you feel like it was a dream
Wake up and smell the roses you fool
What you did was not very cool

A reality check you must endure
For you lost your family to be sure
There is one thing that you can do
To keep the love that you once knew

Go get counseling for that temper inside
That keeps coming on the outside
Seek help and let her know
You love her more then she will ever know

Ask God

Before you succumb to the lust
Ask God for guidance
Look at what you have
Look at what you may lose
Look at what you may destroy
Look at whom you will hurt

Before you indulge
Ask God for strength
Resist the wicked temptation
Resist your inner thoughts
Resist the home breaker
Resist the brief gratification

Before you break your vow
Ask God for help
Pray for strength
Pray for guidance
Pray for resistance
Pray for will power

Before you raise your hand
Ask God for help
Control that thumping thump
Control that vicious voice
Control that agonizing anger
Control that screeching scream

Before you have another drink
Ask God for help
Stop the binge drinking
Stop that tavern run
Stop that afternoon six-pack
Stop for yourself and your family

Don't Do It

Don't do it
Don't have the affair
Don't shatter your life
Don't break your vows
Don't destroy your family

Don't do it
Don't raise your voice in anger
Don't raise you hand in violence
Don't strike the one you love
Don't hurt your family

Brother I feel my own pain
I understand the hurt I caused
Being alone tonight hurts
I cry myself to sleep
I wake up in disbelief

Don't do it
It is not worth it
No matter the pleasure
The pain hurts more
The consequence hurts many

Think Man Think

Think of yourself
Think of your wife
Think of your children
Think of expenses
Think of sadness
Think of loneness
Think man think
Think of cooking
Think of cleaning
Think of laundry
Think of shopping
Think of crying
Think of depression
Think of your life
Think man think

WIN YOUR CHILDREN'S HEART

For children divorce can be devastating
Know that from the beginning
Remember they are so fragile
So please go the extra mile
Do not do anything in malice
For your children will pay the price
Pay the rent/mortgage for God's sake
If you do not, ill will you will make
Take time to spend time when you can
A night out with them you must plan
A movie, a dinner or a board game
The time is all the same
Being with them is what is significant
Knowing that is magnificent
One more thing please
Never give them a feel of unease
Do not put down their mother
They do not want to hear that from another
Yes women, the same is true for you
Putting down the father hurts them too
Let him see them all the time
Anything less is a crime
For the children need both parents
No matter what the currents
Keep the troubles away
They do not want to hear you say
Anything against the women who gave them birth
This would not be seen as mirth
Love them all with all your heart
Love them from the start
And if you have a chance to reconcile
Do it, go the extra mile

It Is Not Your Fault Kids

Sometimes people change
Once they could not be apart
Now they cannot be together
Life changes all the time
Sometimes for the best
Sometimes for the worst
Mommy and Daddy are changing
The shouting is getting louder
The arguments are becoming more frequent
The atmosphere in the house is tense
Mommy and Daddy changed
They once loved being together
Now they cannot live with one another
Nothing you did caused this
Nothing you could have done
Mommy and Daddy are growing apart
They both still love you
Their love for you has not changed
It is difficult for you to understand
Daddy will not be at home anymore
Daddy has his own place
Daddy still loves you
Daddy's love has not changed
You will be living with Mommy
Mommy still loves you
Mommy's love has not changed
Do not blame yourself
Nothing you did caused this
Nothing you could have done

LOVING THAT CHILD

Give her your love
Be there if she wants
Try to offer an olive branch
Along with a dove

Give her the space
Be there if she wants
Try to offer hope
Let her know you are her ace

Give her an embrace
Be there if she wants
Try to offer a grace period
Do not get in her face

Give her a poem
Be there if she wants
Try to offer continuity
Tell her she will not lose her home

Give her time to heal
Be there if she wants
Try to offer counseling
Share with her a meal

Give her your heart
Be there if she wants
Try to console her
Love her from the start

Give her time to adjust
Be there if she wants
Try to make her comfortable
Understanding her needs is a must

Give her a memory
Be there if she wants
Try to sing her that lullaby
Tell her her favorite bedtime story

I Write

I write out of despair
I write to relieve my anguish
I write to educate
I write to prevent more pain
I write to express my feelings
I write to help others

I write to warn you
I write to stop you from going astray
I write to save your marriage
I write to save your children
I write to keep you together
I write to show life after divorce
I write to enlighten you about the aftermath

Adjectives for the Ordeal of Divorce

Appalling
Anguish
Apologetic
Betrayal
Blameworthiness
Bewail
Discredited
Dishonored
Disgraced
Gloomy
Grief
Guilt
Hurtful
Harmed
Humiliated
Lamenting
Lost
Lonely
Mortified
Mangled
Misery
Remorse
Regret
Repentance
Sorrow
Sorry
Shameful
Traumatized
Truncated
Trashed

Part II

Sorrow

Within Her Within Me
Without Each Other

The anger within her is justifiable
The shame within me is unbearable
The rage within her is deserved
The guilt within me is enduring
The pain within her is understandable
The disgrace within me intolerable
The trust within her is missing
The reputation within me is aching
The love within her is confusable
The love within me is consumable
The faith within her is gone
The blame within me is alone
The future within her is lonesome
The world within me is boredom

Both Wondering Why?

Why did she cause the hurt?
Wondering about the undeserving agony
Why did he not forgive?
Wondering why he dismissed a second chance

Why did she cause the crying all day?
Wondering what went wrong?
Why did he not see his faults?
Wondering where the love went wrong

Why did she succumb?
Wondering if there is shared blame
Why did he not see the signs?
Wondering if he was blind

Why did she do it?
Wondering about all those years
Why did he give up so easily?
Wondering about the commitment he had?

Why did he do it?
Wondering about the children's future
Why did he not think of the children?
Wondering about their education

Why did she do it?
Wondering how the mortgage will be paid
Why did she kick him out?
Wondering how she will live

Why did he?
Wondering about why
Why did she?
Wondering about why

BEING

Being alone
It is not fun
I feel like a stone
Beaten by the sun

Being by myself
It is not right
I feel like an elf
Dwarfed by the night

Being unaccompanied
It is not natural
I feel like I lost my need
Humiliated by the betrayal

Being in divorce
It is not fine
I feel like I am in remorse
Restricted from my children's time

Being in court
It is humiliating
I feel like the ball on a tennis court
Battling back and forth is excruciating

SORRY

I am sorry
I am truly sorry
I am truly and honestly sorry
I am truly, honestly and fervently sorry
I am truly, honestly, fervently and remorsefully sorry
I am truly, honestly, fervently, remorsefully and respectfully sorry
I am truly, honestly, fervently, remorsefully, respectfully and
genuinely sorry

BUT

Will you forgive
Will you forgive and forget
Will you forgive, forget and excuse
Will you forgive, forget, excuse and release
Will you forgive, forget, excuse, release and absolve
Will you forgive, forget, excuse, release, absolve and pardon

Alone

I wake up alone
I have breakfast alone
I have my coffee alone
I shower alone
I dress alone
I dine alone
I clean alone
I do the dishes alone
I do the laundry alone
I shop alone
I watch TV alone
I sleep alone
I cry alone

All Alone With Some Hope

Being all alone
Away from my family
After a blunder
Of my own making
What a fool I am
Immorally destroying
A life of everything
To a life of nothing
I feel all alone
Looking forward
I see emptiness
Looking back
I see happiness
So why did I do it
Break my vows
There is no excuse
Just a chance
A hopeful opportunity
To make amends
To establish trust
To vow faithfulness
Forever and ever
Then maybe, just maybe
I will not be alone

I Want Them Back

I do not want to live alone
I want my wife back
I want my children back
I do not want to be separated
I want my life back
I want my love back
I do not want to sleep alone
I want my lover back
I want my partner back
I do not want to die alone
I want my companion back
I want my loved ones back

I Pledge

I pledge, promise, swear and guarantee
That I will remain faithful to you perpetually
That I will regain your trust forever
That I will respect you everlastingly
That I will honor you constantly
That I will always be true to you
That I will love you and you only eternally

Will you accept my pledge?

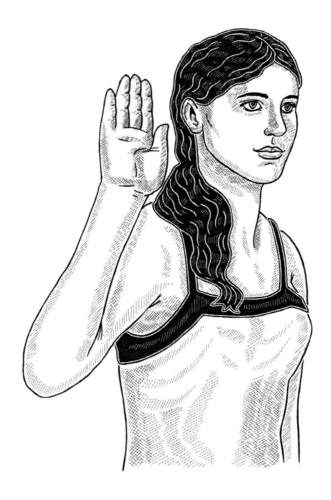

New Start For Two Hearts

The future without my love
Is like death of a dove
Striking the car windshield
Splattered soul that did not yield
Did not yield to temptation
Causing a family destruction
Causing two hearts to split
Split a couple many said fit
Fit for a lifetime so it seemed
Seemed like a life of a dream
Dreaming of reconciliation
Reconcile one heart with a heart
To begin a new start

Adjectives for Rebuilding of Trust

Assurance
Affection
Adoring
Beloved
Believed
Befriend
Caring
Candor
Compassion
Devoted
Dedicated
Determined
Enjoy
Entrust
Expressive
Forgiving
Faithful
Frankness
Hug
Holy
Honesty
Kindness
Kiss
Kindhearted
Listen
Love
Loyalty
Pledge
Promise
Proclamation
Trustworthy
Truthful
Time

LEARNING

Life is a learning experience
We never stop learning
The smartest person yearns for more
Yearns for knowing
Knowing what he does not know

I look at life and learn
Learn from my experiences
Experiences that teach
Teaching me how to live
Live better each day

So I have made a mistake
A mistake that has hurt many
Hurt many of my nearest and dearest
Nearest and dearest to my heart
My heart is sorrowful

Now what have I learned
Learned never to make the same mistake
Learned to be faithful to the one I love
Learned to love and be more compassionate
Compassionate each and every day

I have also learned
Two people need to work together
One may make a mistake
A mistake that should not be made bigger
Bigger when A leads to B

But B should have never come
If the consequence of B was foretold
And A was not corrected to avert B
Correct A before B hurts both
Both parties here are at fault

Correct   **Before**

Rebuilding Hope

What happened to me?
A transgression committed
A heart I have broken
A dream I destroyed
A trust I have shattered
A wife I have wounded
A family I have traumatized

What has happened to me?
A transgression I must never commit
A heart I must repair
A dream I must rebuild
A trust I must regain
A spouse I must love
A family I must preserve

LAYING ASIDE A FEELING

I do not know why
But the feeling inside
Will not fly
Aside I try to lay my pride
But the feeling keeps coming back
For I see a loneliness in this house
It is a feeling that I lack
I try to fly around and bounce
However, without the feeling, I am sad
There is something yearning
Something I once had
Something I feel missing
Will the feeling come anew
And make me stronger in life
Will the feeling renew
My desire for the feeling to strive
I long for the feeling today
Hoping it comes tomorrow
For aside I want to lay
The feeling of sorrow

GUILTY OF BEING HUMAN

I am guilty of being human
I committed a sin
I asked for forgiveness
I received it
Not from my love
But from God

I am guilty of being human
I wanted more then I was given
I asked for compassion
I received it
Not from my love
But from God

I am guilty of being human
I must live with my guilt
I asked for understanding
I received it
Not from my love
But from God

MUTUALITY

It amazes me that life can be so limited
School for two decades
Marriage for another two
Children along the way
Then the mundane sets in
Where is the fun?
You get in a rut
Work, home, sleep
Work, home, sleep
Is there something better?
Which partner needs to make the move?
Which one needs to change the atmosphere?
Does it take one or two?
Mutuality is what love started
Mutuality is what must endure
But when one tries
And the other does not respond
There is something wrong with mutuality
It is gone
Gone from the relationship
And one has to go her separate way
Only to seek that which she lost
That mutuality of respect, love and hope
And when she seeks it
Life begins anew
For her life buzzes with the bees
Sweet moments remove the dullness
Seeking the mutuality that was lost
She learns to love again
Respect and hope are renewed
And life becomes unlimited again.

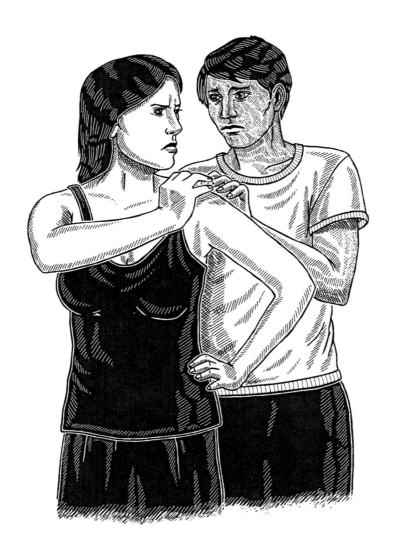

REALLY REALLY ALONE

Never lived alone
Lived with parents through college plus
Married and lived with wife
Now I am living alone

Never did the laundry before
Mother did it when I was at home
Wife did it when I was with her
Now I am doing laundry alone

Never worried about meals
Mother cooked when I was at home
Wife took care of cooking mostly
Now I am cooking alone

Now I am sleeping alone
Now I am doing everything alone
Now I am really really alone

Turning the Wife Into a Witch

You get to a point fellows
When nothing mellows
Your ten minutes late
She shuts the gate

Bring the children home on the dime
She screams all the time
Trying to catch you doing wrong
So she can cry her favorite song

This would not be like this
If you were not remiss
You got caught in a trap
She is going to rap rap rap

Rap you for every little thing
Lower your stature from a king
She will make you feel like a mouse
Already she kicked you out of the house

A scorned women is something to fear
She will act mean even when she says dear
So fellows is it worth it to satisfy your itch
Turning your wife into a witch

VISITATIONS

Visits with the children
How awkward it is
Picking them up from their home
Their home not yours
How distressing it is
When some do not want to come
Seeing them once a week
Trying to act normal
When the pain is inside
Trying to hide it is hard
You go on
You want to give them more
Yet not spoiling them too much
Yet you want to make up for lost time
Spend quality time with them
Do not buy their love
Miss them when you drop them off
Hold back the tears until their gone

I Tried To No Avail

I turned to God
I turned to a priest
I turned to relatives
I turned to friends

I pledged to be true
I was apologetic
I was remorseful
I was lonely

I cried out for help
I received no compassion
I received no love
I received no hope

I tried to reconcile but to no avail
My messengers were rebuked
My agreement to amicability was noted
My sorrow for the hatred

I have given up
Not on the children
Not on my future
Not on my life

You Got What You Wanted

Being free from me is what you wanted
Therefore, your wish has been granted
Being determined you wanted partition
Therefore, broken is our connection

Being insensitive to any reconciliation
Therefore, final is our separation
Being an unforgiving soul
Therefore, we are no longer whole

Being unconcerned for the future
Therefore, you lost the motherly nurture
Being conceited in your abilities
Therefore, you will lose your equities

Being ignorant of what you had
Therefore, you will become sad
Not being regretful for what you have done
Therefore, we are no longer one

Good Father Forever

I will be the best father ever
Their not moving out of my life
I will love them forever
Their happiness is my goal
I will be there for their needs
Their love is my energy
I will keep their lifestyles the same
Their education means everything to me
I will monitor their homework habits
Their future will be secure
I will work hard to assure this
Their love is so important to me
I will secure it by being a good father
Their mother will be respected
I will demand of this of them
Their future will be secure
I will work a million hours to make sure

Part III

Tomorrow

I Will Live

I have felt guilty
I have felt lonely
I have felt like a fool
I have felt sorry for myself

But then I questioned myself
But then I reassessed myself
But then I looked deep into myself
But then I thought about myself

Am I going to wallow in my sorrow?
Am I going to surrender to my depression?
Am I going to lie in a state of shock?
Am I going to die within my soul?

No, I will not feel sorry for myself
No, I will not let this bring me down
No, I will not guilt control my destiny
No, I will not be guided by shame

I will bounce back
I will enjoy life
I will be happy
I will live

Free, Free As I Can Be

Free, free as I can be
To do whatever I want to do
To go wherever I want to go
To explore whatever I want to explore
To play whatever I want to play

Free, free as I can be
To feel whatever I want to feel
To think how I want to think
To invest whatever I want to invest
To work how I want to work

Free, free as I can be
To hug whomever I want to hug
To be hugged by whomever I want to be hugged by
To talk to whomever I want to talk to
To dine with whomever I want to dine with

Free, free as I can be
To search for whomever I want to search
To pursue whomever I want to pursue
To date whomever I want to date
To love whomever I want to love

Looking for Ms. Perfect

No one out there is perfect
I am not perfect
Is there really perfection
Or something close
For me smoking is not
Wanting children is not
Sorry but that is me
Been there done that
My interests are to travel
To enjoy life with someone special
My children are important
So it must be
Passion needs to be a part of life
Holding hands, a smile my way
A hug for no reason at all
Giving and getting
Receiving and remitting
Loving and being loved
There has to be one for me
Keep looking until I find
A perfect one for me

What I Want, What We All Want

I want what I did not get
I want love where there was none
I want one love and only one love
I want my hand held while walking through the woods
I want my cheek stroked while driving in the country
I want my leg rubbed underneath the table at a restaurant
I want a glance from across the room telling me yes
I want a simple affectionate stroke of my hair
I want a smile with a twinkle in her eye just because
I want a playful snowball fight
I want a Jacuzzi bubble bath together
I want to romance my love with oil and roses
I want to cherish the fall foliage arm in arm
I want to show affection anywhere anytime
I want to tease and be teased
I want to travel with her, by her and for her
I want to do what she wants to do
I want to a spontaneous, get up and go approach to life
I want to work to live, not live to work
I want to mutually grow in love and understanding every day

Looking For The Morning Sun

I am going out tonight
I may not be back way before the light
The light of the morning sun
Inside this home I am only one
I cannot wallow
Inside with my sorrow
I must live
Live and of myself give
Give myself the joy of life
For I no longer have a wife
I need to search for the happiness
The happiness I lacked no less
I need the touch of a warm hand
While listening to a favorite band
I need the cuddling in her arms
Feeling all the beauty of her charms
I am searching for the one
Who will make me feel I won
Won the love that I can reciprocate to
Then and only then can I be true
True to my self and my mate
So I am searching for that ultimate date
The date that will be my last one
The one that will lead me to the morning sun

Enjoying The Patter Inside

The rapid patter beating inside
Sings gently into the night
Feeling the warmth of the air
The patter prays to the heavens
Stimulation enhances the mood
Secure in love
The rhythm embraces the moment
Believing it will last a lifetime
The romance endures
The intellect is kept at bay
For if summoned
It has to assess the being
Beyond the affection
But now at this juncture
The physicality is delightful
The moment is frozen in time
Enjoying more with every beat
Beating faster and faster
Uncontrolled at this point in time

I Will

I will meet the one for me
I will see him in my dreams
I will be summoned by my heart
I will be guided by my mind
I will learn from my mistakes
I will change for the better
I will be faithful on all accounts
I will be a spontaneous lover
I will be a gracious giver
I will take the time to smell the roses
I will count my blessings each day
I will look into his eyes and be thankful
I will tell him my feelings
I will ask him for his feelings
I will be considerate of him
I will affectionately stroke his hair
I will give him that enchanting glance
I will talk to him about everything
I will touch him with compassion
I will be his best friend
I will cherish our love

LIFE IS ALL RELATIVE

Life is all relative
You do what you can to live
When a bowl of cherries life throws
You can act like the crows
And only eat the crumb
No you must not succumb
Take charge of the life you face
You can look for that ace
In one of the pits
Or you can see what fits
The pits you must spit out
Eat only the fruit no doubt
Everyone has different strokes
For me, I cannot be with one that smokes
So you move on down the road
For you do not want a toad
The crumbs you do not need
Your minds judgment you should heed
Your heart may desire the pleasure
But your mind must take measure
Measure everything relatively
Is everything about her fittingly?
Does she fit in your environment?
Will the negative lead to resentment?
Or will the positive outweigh?
Giving you love along the way

Looking For The Right One

Looking for the right one
Is like staring into the sun
If you look long enough, you will go blind
Then the one you seek, you will never find
Search to your heart's content
However, know to what extent
Your heart will control your judgment
Leaving your mind without fulfillment
When your mind and heart meet
In the clouds will be your feet
Nevertheless, be careful and let your mind control
Control your heart and soul
The feeling of love is heartwarming
It comes without any warning
But when it arrives
Your mind has to surmise

Is she the one for you?
Can it really be true?
Let your heart take over a bit
And let your mind a while sit
Let your heart fly
Taking you and her to the sky
Then as you see the skyline
Determine if she is fine
Fine enough to live with forever
Knowing that you will leave her never
Your mind must make the decision
Navigating away from a collision
Of heart and mind going blind
But rather of heart and mind that bind

COULD SHE BE THE ONE

As she walked into the restaurant bar
I gazed at her from afar
She looked absolutely stunning
Just what I was expecting
When she got closer to me
I could then see
Why the beauty of her eyes of blue
Surrendered my heart in two
We had a drink while we got acquainted
Feeling comfortable, we got situated
We then moved to dine
Everything seemed just fine
We talked about everything and anything
So much in common, it was amazing
I met my match when it comes to the police stories
Hers were more dramatic realities
We talked about religion and politics
On a first date they do not mix
But we both felt comfortable
As we sat, ate and chatted at our table
Chatted about everything under the sun
So wonderful I believe we both had fun
The check came and she wanted to pay
And I said I am a gentleman no way
We were the last couple still sitting
I do not think we were thinking of leaving
But like all good things the evening had to end
And I believe I have found a new friend
We walked outside and I gave her my poetry book
And then she gave me that look
She walked to her car and her scanners
And then I realized what happened to my manners
I ran to her and walked her to her car
I had the most wonderful time by far

When Love Meets Intellect

When I find her
I will know she is the one
My heart will love
My mind will take measure
Both will know together
If my heart steals the show
My mind will take control
It will assess the feelings
Looking for hurt in the horizon
Seeing none it will allow the beat to go on
Seeing pain it will gently walk away
When love meets intellect, it is wonderful
Together they embrace her
And a new tenderness emerges
More affection then with just love
More happiness in conversation
Knowing each other intimately
With her they will communicate
About love, arts, politics, you name it
The mind will enjoy what the heart desires
The heart will love what the mind encounters
Together they will know she is the one

INTO MY BEING

You are not here
And I am not there
Miles are between us
A plane ride away
Yet the hearts are closer
Closer then ever
Metaphysically I see you
And I feel you
Your voice echoes beyond
Beyond cyber space
And into my being

You are not here
And I am not there
A smile I cannot see
A glance I cannot notice
Yet I see your warm eyes
Eyes I have come to adore
Emotionally I feel you
And my heart sees you
Your heart beats a message
A message of hope
And into my being

Waiting For the Call

She sounds so interesting
Talking the night through
We talk about everything
Even a joke or two
We felt comfortable from the start
An ear that listens and hears
Each consoling the other's heart
And comforting each other's fears
The innuendos are witty
The charm is heartfelt
We are far apart what a pity
The appeal makes me melt
Calling her is the highlight
Of the day that lingers
Waiting for the call all day and night
No more chatting with the fingers
I think she is wonderful
Does she think the same
Maybe life can be plentiful
Maybe meeting is our aim

MAKING HER FEEL LIKE A QUEEN

Of course I write poems that are real
I write when a pretty lady has appeal
When I see a pretty smile
Like yours, I go the extra mile
Silly me, I should have also said wonderful
For that smile is so plentiful
Plentiful enough to feel it through miles of spaces
Feel it like a good poker hand, two aces
Aces wild to start
Can two aces have one heart
I do not know the answer, do you
Maybe we can chat and see if its true
E-mail me at ******@yahoo.com soon
E-mail me at high noon
We can stare each other down
Maybe I can make you wear a crown
Yes I can make you feel like a queen
Cause a King I am, feeling real keen
Waiting eagerly to hear from you
My heart is beating fast, is yours too

WHAT IS IT?

What is it about you?
That caused me to miss you
I hardly know who you are
You could have fallen from a star
Dropped right into my heart
A beauty from the start

What is it about your charm?
That set off an alarm
Caused me to think
Think with a wink
A wink in your direction
Could it be a love connection?

What is it about your beauty?
That mesmerizes me you little cutie
A cutie with the silky hair
Hair that catches the breeze in the air
Warms it in her heart
Then releases it through a love dart

What is it about your character?
That is blessed by our Maker
A Maker who has given you a gift
Blessed your soul and mind
Made you really really kind
Given you a new sensation
Leaving you in adulation

DRENCHED LOVERS

Does the Moon wink at the Earth?
Or does it smile at the Stars?
The Moon spins
Sneaking a glance during the night
Sometimes partially hidden
Sometimes fully exposed
Then it hides
Looking to the heavens for guidance
The Stars sparkle in response
The Moon turns to the Earth and smiles
The attraction creates a tidal wave
Two lovers are drenched
As they embrace along the beach
The Sun seeing all
Warms them kindly
Giving them the Moon and the Stars

THE BUTTERFLY FLUFFS HER WINGS

The butterfly has landed on my shoulder
I hold out my hand and it floats to my palm
It tickles my veins and my blood flows with passion
A warm breeze caresses and the butterfly fluffs her wings
The whisper of the night sings
The tone beckons a kiss and an embrace follows
The touch of her soft smooth skin is engaging
As she now floats to my heart and into my spirit
I smile knowing my senses are comforted
As my fingers flow through her silky wings of hair
I hold her closer and tighter
Desiring to hold time still
I release her to see if she will fly and leave
But she stays, knowing she is mine and only mine

IN THE MORNING

Your beauty in the morning
Must be so glowing
I can see your eyes
Bright, beautiful and just the right size
Your warmth penetrates cyber space
I wish I were your ace
Being next to you would make my heart true
It will come true, as I will be with you
Maybe not today
But it will come someday
I will look into your bright eyes
And I will take off to the skies
Soaring with love, respect and warmth
As our love enhances in growth
I would caress your body
Touching you softly and boldly
Feeling you from head to toe
Then in your ear I will blow
Sweet warm air full of love
Then take you on a flight like a dove
We will fly to the sea
Smell the breeze as we see
Feel the warmth of the moment
Making little comment
Just relaxing in the arms of each other
Not wanting to be with another
A kiss of your sweet lips
A touch of your luscious hips
A tongue on your nipple
As my hand sends a ripple
A ripple down your spine
All the way down the line
I touch you there
You look at me and stare
Your eyes are smiling

My heart is pounding
You take me in
I say wait a min
I tease you some more
We caress evermore
I kiss your neck
Then give you a soft peck
You turn me over and around
My heart begins to pound
We are in the groove
As we make every move
The moment is just right
As the morning begins to bright
The sun glows in the morning ray
As love is invited to stay
What a wonderful feeling
As you begin screaming
Passion overflows
As the wind blows
In comes a warm breeze
This is a picture frame to freeze
Freeze it forever
Releasing it never

A Song Resurrects Lost Emotions

The song is one that I have not heard for decades
The words bring back feelings lost in time
I sing along as her beauty reminds me of the lyrics
Lovely words resurrect emotions buried deep inside
Surfacing with the chorus so long forgotten
A tear of happiness reminds me of what was found
A buried treasure located in a song
The hymn repeats and we dance
The steps come back, two steps then three
I twirl her as my life spins anew
Dormant feelings come alive
My ears perk up to listen intensely
My fingers sense her silky hair
My over dry lips are moistened by a kiss
My heart sings the words of love once again

Safa

She Is the One

Wise Advice

I have always advised the young at heart
That they will marry from the start
The one that captures their mind first
Rather then their heart that does thirst
And so I have thus experienced such
The words I preached have come to me as much
For I have found her days before I publish
Send this book to the press and finish
But I would be remiss
To end here and miss
Miss the opportunity and the chance
To explain to the reader about our romance
To not give a conclusion to these rhymes
Would be the highest of all crimes
So here it is for all to know
The conclusion of the show

Chatting Then Meeting

The story started in a world known as cyber space
We chatted and talked not face to face
So much in common, we did find
That a connection was in both our mind
Through the night for hours at a time
We said being apart was a crime
And so I packed my bag and flew
Flew to her on Jet-Blue
On the plane I did write
This poem entitled First Encounter which is proper and right

First Encounter

In flight anticipation
Of the first encounter
Landing soon
Awkward cultural moment
Do we hug?
Do I kiss her cheek?
Thrilled expectation
What is she thinking?
Respect calls for shaking hands
And, so it shall be

Corny Story?

But, wait and listen to this story
You may think it is rather corny
Yes, love may be silly in every way
Silly in the way lovers act and say
I landed at the airport known for JFK
In anticipation my heart said to me hurry if you may
My mind did reply
Take it easy Sly
Be cool and patient
Show a little restraint
Well, she waited in the car for me
As the luggage I did not see
For my suitcase did not make it to the baggage claim
So I signed a claim by signing my name

Eyes That Sparkle

Then I went to see Safa in the car
She looked more stunning in person by far
And as we drove off away from the airport
Sunglasses covered her eyes of sort
I asked for the sunglasses to be removed
And behold I noticed the eyes that moved
Moved me as I saw them live at first sight
Sparkling hazel green color in the light
Her smile mesmerized my soul
As onward, the car did stroll
We went to the hotel to check me in
Then we went for a spin

Dining At Crossing

Dining for lunch at Underhills Crossing
As our chat with the waiter was smashing
David is a German/Puerto Rican with a Jewish twinge
I joked that Safa was my daughter as she did cringe
Cringe with laughter as we finished our dine
Then a walk we took to get further acquainted in time
As I went to check on the luggage back at the hotel
You may be asking me, pray tell
Well, the luggage was not there yet
Although we had plans set
Just before Safa came to pick me up around nine
The luggage arrived just fine

Beautiful and Delightful

Soon thereafter, that evening on that day
We crossed the bay
To New Jersey over the GW Bridge so we could dance
To dance at the Nile Restaurant and exchange many a glance
The belly dancer used fans which was beautiful
I must say Safa's dancing was more delightful
As we dined there was a moment
I did want to comment
But I left it alone until I could write
Write it tonight

Expressed Hope

She gave that look
Accompanied by a smile
Her eyes expressed hope
I looked deep into them
I saw a future

In the wee hours of the morning we drove in the dark
As she dropped me off by the hotel as we did park
Take note, I still have not held her hand thus far
However, I did give her a hug before she departed with her car

Good Mood

When the next day I saw her in the light
I continued the hug that lasted all night
To break the ice and the slight tension
May I mention?
A kiss on the cheek I did give that felt good
A spontaneous setting of the mood
Then off we went to Manhattan by train
It was such a beautiful day, glad it did not rain

Walking, Talking, Praying

From Grand Central Station we did walk
Hand holding hand, finally, as we did talk
Our hearts were getting closer I could feel
Everything was happening so fast, was it real?
A surreal moment at St. Patrick Cathedral did occur
As we both lit a candle without any demur
I prayed to God and thanked Him for Safa's presence
I also prayed to be a part of her essence
We sat in a pew together
And we prayed next to each other
Is it strange that on the first day we meet?
That we step into a church with both our feet
We exited the Cathedral and walked along
Within my heart, there was a song

Pair to Wear

Her sunglasses were broken
And as a small token
We went into Fossil and purchased a pair
A pair of glasses so we both can wear
Spontaneously, we wanted to go to the Statue of Liberty
To come to NY and not see the Old Lady would be a tragedy
But the taxi-cab driver, who should have known
That the Old Lady closes at 3:30 pm on its own

Truly Purely Magical

It was Sunday, 5:00 pm now
And oh how
I did not want the end of the day to be practical
As it turned out, it was magical
We went back to the hotel by way of the subway
Planning our evening was on my mind throughout the day
Had I written it out as a play
I do not think it would have been better that day
The following is what actually happened at night
Then I woke up and wrote this poem when up came the light

AN UNUSUAL ENCOUNTER TEACHES

Two lovers were in search of a bottle of wine
To share as part of a setting for a romantic dine
Searching a remote New York town all around
Nowhere could an open store be found
When an encounter pursued by chance
A wonderful lady was asked at a glance
A gracious offering to the lovers she made
Amazed, the appreciative couple accepted her aid
To her home she did escort
And she searched for the best bottle of port
The bottle of Brunello Di Montalcino spirited the mood
Arousing the sensations of the food
However, this is not all to this encounter
For these strangers learned things can be sounder
Sounder between two peoples far away
Fighting each other every day
Why must this be?
Can they not see?
We are all God's children living to be free
In a land along the Mediterranean Sea
You see the lovers are a Palestinian pair
And the wonderful lady is Jewish who did care
Care to offer her generosity
To fulfill a night of intimacy
Still, it really goes beyond all that
It tells us that if the two sides just sat
Sat down and felt the warmth of the lady that night
Embrace each other and talk to bring forth light
The light shining down from God on all the land
The land of Abraham, Jesus and Mohammad with all its sand

A REAL MEAL

I printed this poem and framed it with a frame
Then Safa and I delivered the poem to Sarita, that's her name
Before we delivered the poem, however, Safa suggested coffee
She would make it at her home--it was rather tasty
She also suggested a meal
Mloukhia was one of my favorites for real
And so we cooked together in her kitchen happily
I peeled the garlic and squeezed the lemon joyfully
Together we shared our third meal
Stupendous was the food and the feel
The feeling that Safa has everything I want
My mind began to take measure, to take count
After delivering the poem, we went to the park for a walk
Along the way, we continued the talk
We talk with ease about anything
We talk at length about everything

REACTION TO PASSION

But there is more magic to this tale
Something else happened that surprised us without fail
I would need to be at the airport in several hours
The time left I wanted it to be special, all ours
I looked for an Italian restaurant to make a lasting memory
As I drove in search of such a luxury
We stopped at this small restaurant with an Italian name
From the outside it is ordinary, just the same
The same restaurant with the same style
But as Safa waited outside and I entered with a smile
My senses did enhance
They started to do a dance
I cannot describe the sensational joy
That my senses did enjoy
The smell of the eggplant, bakala and salads were vibrant
Why I could go on and rant, rant and rant
The smell came from a dazzling buffet table
Dazzling with colors of food so balanced and stable
Wow, was our reaction
We have found this place of passion
I asked if the establishment
Was open for nourishment
No was the answer as they were having
A Grand Opening
So, they invited Safa and me in
Wonderful folks that made me spin
Spin in disbelief about what is said
About New Yorker's attitudes and what I have been fed
The attitude that New Yorker's are rude
Is not at all true, rather it is crude

Leaving With A Feeling

Two days before I flew
I had a feeling, I knew
I knew Safa was the one
My heart she had won
Now I am on the plane
Reflecting just the same
About what I wrote
Two days before when my heart did vote

WHAT A FEELING

Oh! What a feeling
She is stealing
My heart taken ---- away

Oh! I can't believe it
I really feel it
My heart melting ---- away

Oh! It is amazing
She is appealing
My heart charmed ---- away

Oh! It is wonderful
I feel sensational
My heart content ---- today

Oh! It is breathtaking
She is captivating
My heart delighted ----today

Oh! It is thrilling
I awake thinking
My heart happy ---- today

Again, I wrote something about Safa on Jet-Blue
Right before we met as I flew
Reasoning why I am on my way
To see her that day

A Self-Assured Woman

Much like a pretty flower
A self-assured woman knows her beauty
Vibrant like a rose
Her cheekbone illuminates
Succulent like morning dew on a tulip
Her lips vividly sizzle with moisture
Adoring like lilies in the field
Her hair shines giving her an added glow
Sparkling like a sea of daisies
Her eyes twinkle a confident assurance

Further Wondering About Earlier

I wondered further
About the poems written earlier
About the mind and heart
Are they together like a piece of art
Today is Monday
And on the day we met---Saturday
I did something dramatic
At least it was never before automatic

Adding Her Name

I added her name to my dictionary
Never did it before
Safa is not underlined anymore
This program knows her name
What does it mean?
I know, I know
She has entered
My mind and heart

The One---Done

So agreement has been reached by my two parts
Affection flows to combine our hearts
As our minds also meet
Combining two hearts that beat
My search is done
Safa is the one!

LaVergne, TN USA
18 February 2010
173572LV00002B/258/P